OXFORD TO BLETCHLEY

including Verney Junction to Banbury

Vic Mitchell and Keith Smith

MP Middleton Press

EVOLVING THE ULTIMATE RAIL ENCYCLOPEDIA

Cover picture: Speedy express services to Cambridge were provided experimentally, bringing fame to the route. The DMU is at the Oxford terminus of the LMSR on 17th September 1938. (Milepost 92½)

Published July 2005

ISBN 1 904474 57 8

© Middleton Press, 2005

Design Deborah Esher

Published by
         Middleton Press
         Easebourne Lane
         Midhurst, West Sussex
         GU29 9AZ
Tel: 01730 813169
Fax: 01730 812601
Email: info@middletonpress.co.uk
www.middletonpress.co.uk

Printed & bound by Biddles Ltd, Kings Lynn

CONTENTS

INDEX

ACKNOWLEDGEMENTS

We are very grateful for the assistance received from many of those mentioned in the credits also to P.G.Barnes, A.E.Bennett, W.R.Burton, L.Crosier, G.Croughton, D.Hanson, J.B.Horne, N.Langridge, D.Lovett, Dr J.S.Manners, Mr D. and Dr S.Salter, M.Turvey and particularly our ever supportive wives, Barbara Mitchell and Janet Smith.

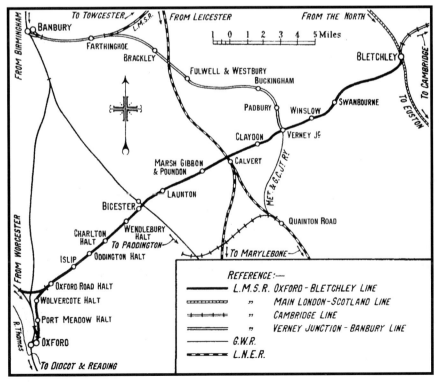

I. Route map in 1930. The line south of Verney Junction has the pre-1923 ownership shown.

GEOGRAPHICAL SETTING

The route is almost entirely on an outcrop of Oxford Clay, which runs parallel to the Chiltern Hills. It crosses few watercourses of note, except in the Oxford area, these being described in that section of the album.

The line is remarkably straight and has no steep gradients of any length, except at its east end near Swanbourne, where it passes over a watershed more than 500ft above sea level.

The only mineral of economic value on the route was clay, used for brickmaking.

The branch traverses various limestones between Buckingham and Banbury, reaching a summit at the junction with the Towcester line. From Buckingham to Brackley, the route climbs close to the River Ouse and in its final few miles it descends into the valley of the River Cherwell.

The maps are to the scale of 25ins to 1 mile, with north at the top, unless otherwise indicated.

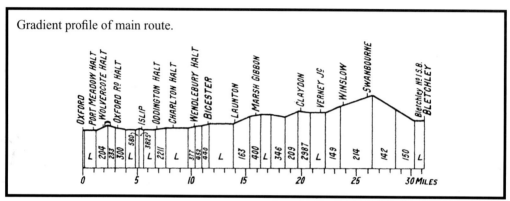

Gradient profile of main route.

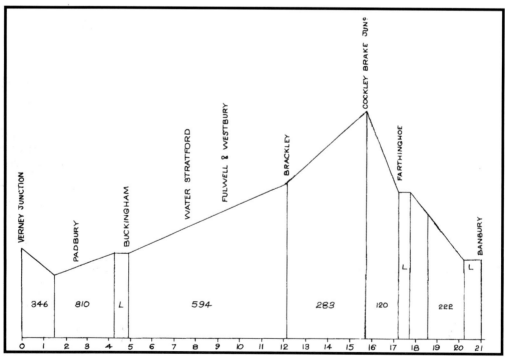

HISTORICAL BACKGROUND

The first line in the area was that of the London & Birmingham Railway, which began operation in the Bletchley area in 1838. It became part of the London & North Western Railway in 1846.

Oxford had been reached by Great Western Railway trains using a branch from Didcot in 1844. These services continued north to Banbury in 1850 and west to Evesham in 1853.

The Buckinghamshire Railway was formed in 1847 to build a line from Bletchley to Oxford, with a branch to Banbury via Brackley. The former was opened from Bletchley to Islip on 1st October 1850 and the latter on 1st May of that year. Trains ran to an independent terminus in Oxford from 20th May 1851.

There were three other routes in the area covered by this album. A line north from Aylesbury reached Verney Junction in 1868 and carried passengers until 1936. The main line from Marylebone crossed our route near Calvert from 1898 until 1966. Still in use is Bicester's second railway, which was opened by the GWR in 1910.

The LNWR became a constituent of the London Midland & Scottish Railway in 1923 and this formed the London Midland Region of British Railways in England in 1948. The Oxford - Bicester section was transferred to the Western Region in 1958. Diesel units were introduced on the route on 2nd November 1959.

Bletchley - Oxford passenger trains were withdrawn on 1st January 1968, the route remaining open for freight. A Bicester - Oxford service was restored on 11th May 1987 and Islip was reopened on 15th May 1989.

The Bicester - Bletchley section was technically "mothballed" on 31st May 1993, but the section west of Claydon Junction was reopened on 24th January 1994 for waste traffic to Calvert. The remainder was nominally still open ten years later, but unused.

Banbury Branch

The line opened slightly ahead of the main route, as already stated, and was also built by the Buckinghamshire Railway. It was joined at Cockley Brake Junction by the Northampton & Banbury Junction Railway in 1872. The Stratford-upon-Avon & Midland Junction Railway took this over in 1910; it was closed to passengers in 1951 and to freight in 1953.

The Bletchley - Banbury service was operated by British Railways' first single diesel railcars from 13th August 1956, but passenger service was withdrawn between Buckingham and Banbury on 2nd January 1961. However, it remained open as a through freight route until 1963, carrying much ironstone and cattle traffic.

The Verney Junction - Buckingham section lost its passenger service on 7th September 1964, goods continuing until 5th December 1966.

PASSENGER SERVICES

Down trains running on at least five days per week are considered in this section. In the early years there were usually five weekday trains, with one on Sundays. By the late 1860s, the weekday figure was six, this increasing to eight within 20 years.

Steam railmotors were introduced between Bicester and Oxford in October 1905, these providing six trips in addition to the six trains from Bletchley. The figures were four and six in 1920, still with just one on Sundays

Reorganisation in 1930 brought substantial improvements, with four semi-fast and five stopping trains, plus an 8.10am up from Bicester; there were three calling at most stations on Sundays.

The wartime timetable of 1944 offered only six weekday and two Sunday services, mostly all-stations trains. This improved to eight and two by 1951, but the extra from Bicester was withdrawn. Prior to withdrawal, the diesel service was the best ever with ten arrivals at Oxford, but weekdays only.

When the line reopened to Bicester, there were three trains weekdays only in the peak hours, with an extra on Saturdays. A weekday service of seven trains per day was introduced in May 1989, but no Sunday trains were provided.

Banbury Branch

For more than forty years, most departures from Bletchley for Oxford carried portions for Banbury, although in some years one would terminate at Brackley. There were one or two on Sundays, but they were not usually part of an Oxford train. From 1905, most weekday trains were also running independently and numbered four to Banbury, plus one to Brackley. By 1920, the figures were four and two, but there were no Sunday trains.

From about 1933 to the end, there were only two or three weekday trains, with one on Sundays in some years. The Towcester route offered an extra two trains to Farthinghoe residents bound for Banbury until 1951.

Dieselisation in 1956 brought an improvement to six trains, but weekdays only, to Banbury, with three extra to Buckingham. A change there was necessary on some journeys, as steam trains were still partly used east thereof.

OXFORD, BANBURY, BUCKINGHAM, WINSLOW, and BLETCHLEY.—London and North Western

Table 1 (top): Week Days / Sndys / Line Street Sts.

Fares — From Oxford, Fm. Banbury, From Worcester, p. 25. The classes refer to the Branch Line only.

Stations (down): Oxford (Rooley Rd) dep, Islip, Bicester, Launton, C'aydon, Banbury* dep, Farthinghoe, Brackley, Buckingham, Verney Junction 117, Winslow, Swanbourne, Bletchley J. 110, 115

114 LIVERPOOL dep, 114 M'CHSTER LndnR., 114 BRMNGHAM NwSt., 121 PETERBRO, 110 LONDON (Vic.), 110 „ (Kensington), 110 „ (Broad St), 110 „ (Euston), Fm Yarmth, Norwich & Cambdg, 89, & below

115 LONDON (Euston) sr, 115 „ (Broad St.) „, 115 „ (Kensington) „, 115 „ (Victoria) „, 121 PETERBRO, 121 BIRMINGHAM, 111 CHESTER, 111 MANCHESTER, 111 LIVERPOOL

Bletchley Junc. dep, Swanbourne, Winslow, Verney Junction 117, Buckingham, Brackley, Farthinghoe, Banbury* 13, 21, Claydon, Launton, Bicester, Islip [21, 24, 113], Oxford (Rooley R.) ar

Notes: a 3rd class to the North, leaving Bletchley at 9 40 mrn.; also to the Bedford Branch. b 3rd class from Oxford to Chester, Birkenhead, Liverpool, Warrington, and Manchester, changing at Rugby into the 7 40 mrn. Train from London; also to Midland Line, Hull, Newcastle, and North Eastern Line. c 3rd class to inter-mediate Stations between Bletchley and London. d 3rd class to London. e 3rd class to Stations between Winslow and Oxford. f 3rd class to the North, leaving Bletchley at 9 40 mrn.; also to the Bedford Branch and Stations up to Cambridge. g 3rd class from all Stations South of Bletchley to Oxford. h 3rd class from all Stations between Wolverhampton and Bletchley (Bletchley excepted) to Oxford and Banbury. j 3rd class to Banbury. j 3rd class to Oxford. k 3rd class from Birkenhead at 11 mrn., Chester 12 5 aft., Liverpool 10½ mrn., and Warrington 11 13 mrn. to Oxford. l 3rd cl. to London, arr. at 8¼ aft. * Melton Road.

June 1869

OXFORD, BANBURY, WINSLOW, and BLETCHLEY.—London and North Western.

Table 2 (middle): Down. — Week Days / Sundays

Stations: Rooley R. Sts., Oxford dep, Islip, Bicester, Launton (Fndn), Marsh Gibbon, Claydon, Verney Junc., Winslow arr; Banbury* dep, Frthingho, Brackley, Fulwell, Buckingham, Padbury, Verney Junc., Winslow arr; Winslow dep, Swanbourne, Bletchley 164 arr, Bedford, 200 CHESTER, 224 M'CHSTER, 165 L'pool (LS)

Line St. Sts., 163 L'pool Ld, 224 CHESTER, 202 M'CHSTER, Bedford, 164 L'don (E), Bletchley d, Swanbourne, Winslow, Verney Jn. a, Verney Jd, Padbury, Bckngham, Fulwell, Brackley, Frthinghe, Bnbry* arr; Verney Jn. a, Claydn (Fnd), Mrsh Gbbn, Launton, Bicestr, Islip, Oxford (R.R.) ar

Notes: a Stops to set down on informing Guard. b Passengers from Banbury Line change at Winslow, on Saturdays. c Leaves London at 7 10 aft. d Stops by signal to take up for Oxford Branch.

September 1885

July 1906

BLETCHLEY, WINSLOW, VERNEY JUNCTION, BUCKINGHAM, BANBURY, and OXFORD.—London and North Western.

Table 3 (bottom): Week Days / Suns.

Miles from Bletchley.

Euston Station: 384 LONDON dep, 392 LIVERPOOL (Lime S.), 392 MANCHESTER (Lon.R.), 393 BIRMINGHAM (NewSt)

Bletchley dep, Swanbourne, Winslow, Verney Junction 373 arr; Verney Junction dep, Padbury, Buckingham, Fulwell and Westbury, Brackley*, Farthinghoe 499, Banbury † 57; Verney Junction dep, Claydon, Marsh Gibbon and Poundon, Launton, Bicester, Islip, Oxford § 1, 41, 51, 62 arr

Rewley Road Station: Oxford dep, Islip, Bicester, Launton, Marsh Gibbon and Poundon, Claydon, Verney Junction 373 arr; Banbury † dep, Farthinghoe 499, Brackley, Fulwell and Westbury, Buckingham, Padbury, Verney Junction arr; Verney Junction dep, Claydon, Marsh Gibbon, Swanbourne, Bletchley 384 arr; 384 BIRMINGHAM (NewS.) ar, 385 MANCHESTER (Lo.Rd.), 385 LIVERPOOL (Line S.), 393 London (Euston Stn.)

NOTES.
a Stops to take up for the Banbury Line.
B Stops by Signal to take up for the Oxford Line.
b Leaves at 7 10 aft. on Saturdays.
c Stops if required to set down, and to take up for beyond Bletchley.
c Notice to be given to the Guard at Crewe to set down at Bletchley.
* Except Saturdays.
g Stops if required to take up.
h Arrives 3 10 mrn. on Sundays.
n Arrives 2 58 mrn. on Sundays.
o Through-Carriage, London to Banbury.
* Thursdays only.
* About 1½ miles to the Great Central Station.
† Merton Street Station.
§ Rewley Road Station.

"Halts" at Wendlebury, Charlton, Oddington, Oxford Road, and Wolvercote between Bicester and Oxford.

Table 1 — June 1920

BLETCHLEY, VERNEY JUNCTION, BUCKINGHAM, BANBURY, and OXFORD.—London and North Western.

	Down.	Week Days.														Sundays.
		mrn	mrn	mrn				aft	aft	aft	aft	aft	aft	aft	mrn
Miles from Bletchley	324 London (Euston)..dep.		6 45	..	7 35	9 35	1155	1155	2 52	5 3	45	4 0	5 25		9 30
	332 Liverpool (Lime S.) ,,	12 15	..	2 35		7 50		11 0	1140		2 10				12 5
	332 Manchester (Lon R.) ,,	12 a 5	..			7 15		10 0	12 5		2 5				12 5
	333 Birmingham (New St) ,,	12 15	..	7 30		8 45		1125	2 5		3 50				8 30
	356 & Cambridge ,,			7 37			1050	1050	1 45	1 45		4 10			aft
	Bletchley ....dep.	8 15	8 35	10 15		12 10	1220	1 20	1 35	4 5	4 35	4 50	5 30	6 57	7 10	1 15
5	Swanbourne	8 25	8 45	10 15		12 20	1231	1 30	1 44	4 15	4 43	5 0	5 40	7	7 22	
7	Winslow	8 30	8 51	10 23		12 25	1238	1 35	1 55	4 20	4 50	5 5	5 46	7	12 7	1 39
9	Verney Junction 314. arr.	8 37	8 58	10 32		12 33	1245	1 42	2 1	4 57		5 19	5 54	7 19	7 35	1 50
—	Verney Junction....dep.	8 39		10 43			1247		2 2			5 20		5 57	720	
11	Padbury	8 47		10 50			1256		2 8			5 26		6 2	7 26	
13	Buckingham ...... arr.	8 54		10 59			1 2		2 14			5 32		6 6	7 32	
	{dep.	8 55		11 1					2 16			5 35		6 7	7 33	
18	Fulwell and Westbury ,,	9 6		11 12					2 26			5 46		6 18	7 45	
21	Brackley * 498	9 u25		11 20		1127			2 33			5 53		6 25	7 53	
26	Farthinghoe 321	9 40				1142			2 48			6 6		8 7		
30	Banbury† 43.62.66 arr.	9 50				1152			2 58			6 15		8 16		
—	Verney Junction ....dep.		9 0	10 37			12 37		1 43		4 58				7 36	1 55
11	Claydon		9 5	10 42			12 42		1 47		5 3				7 44	2 3
15	Marsh Gibbon and Poundon ,,		9 10	10 51			12 51		1 56		5 13				7 55	2 12
17	Launton		9 22	10 57			12 57		1 2		5 19				8 1	2 18
19	Bicester †§ 62, 66	9 15		11 4		1120	1 3		1 52	2	5 25				8 7	2 25
25	Islip†‡ .... [79	9 38	32	9 42	11 16		1139	1 16		2 42	20	5 38		6 19		8 24	2 39
31	Oxford §41, 62, 66. arr.	8 48		9 55	11 29		1157	1 29		2 22	2 33	5 51		6 37		8 38	2 55

b Arrives 7 28 aft. on Saturdays.   § Rewley Road Station.
d Leaves at 10 30 aft. on Sundays.   t Leaves at 10 aft. on Sundays.   ‖ Over 1 mile to Great Western Sta.

Table 2 — January 1944

BLETCHLEY, VERNEY JUNCTION, BUCKINGHAM, BANBURY, BICESTER, and OXFORD

	Down	Week Days											Sundays		
		mrn	mrn	mrn	mrn	mrn	aft	aft	aft	E aft	S aft	mrn	mrn	mrn	
Miles from Bletchley	463 London (Euston)..dep.		6 45	..	1040	1135	12 15	3 F6	..	7 30	7 15	12 30	11 35	11 35	
	424 Liverpool (L St) ,,	12 2	1230	..	8 15			1020		5 25	5 25	12 30			
	424 Manchester (L Rd) ,,	12 5			8 0			1110		5 35	5 35	12 20	10 35	10 35	
	425 Birmingham (N St) ,,	9u20		6u57	9 0		10u25	2 35		7 47	7 47				
	426 Rugby .... ,,	3 49			7u15		11u15	3 40		6 30	6 30		11 24	11 24	
	469 Cambridge .... ,,				9 30		1125			6 15	6 15		9 50	9 50	
	Bletchley ....dep.	5 15		8 9	9 5	12 15	1 20	2 13		10 17	1017	8 45	1 7	1 10	
5	Swanbourne			8 19	9 15	12 25	1 30	2 23		10 28	1028	8 55	1 17	1 20	
7	Winslow	5 31		8 26	9 21	12 30	1 35	2 28		10 33	1033	9 5	1 23	1 36	
9	Verney Junction .. arr.			8 31	9 26	12 35	1 40	2 33				9 5	1 28	1 40	
—	Verney Junction ..dep.			8 34				2 34					1 29		
11	Padbury			8 39				2 39					1 34		
14	Buckingham {arr.			8 45				2 45					1 40		
	{dep.			8 49				2 47					1 42		
18	Fulwell and Westbury A			8 58				2 56					1 51		
21	Brackley 830			9 9				3 3					1 57		
26	Farthinghoe. 685 [136			9 17				3 14					2 7		
30	Banbury C 98, 103. arr.			9 25				3 22					2 17		
—	Verney Junction ..dep.			9 27	12 37	1 41			5 50			9 6	1 41		
11	Claydon			9 32	12 40	1 44			5 53				1 44		
15	Marsh Gibbon & Poundon ,,	5 45		9 38	12 48	1 52					1041		1 52		
17	Launton			9 42	1252	1 56			6 6			9 22	1 57		
19	Bicester B 98, 103	6u58		9 48	12 57	2X2			6 12			9 28	2X19		
25	Islip ..... [103, 116	6 40		9 58	1 7	2X11			6 23			9 38	2 20		
31	Oxford G 48, 63, 98. arr.	6 51	8 30	10 9	1 18	2X22			6 34		11 13	1115	9 49	2 31	

A 1½ miles to Finmere
^ Arr 2 2 aft.
B Over 1 mile to G.W. Sta.
^ Arr 1 50 afton Sats
C Merton Street
§ Sunday morns only
d Via Northampton (Castle). Dep. 12 16 aft on Sats.
E or E Except Saturdays
F Dep † 30 aft on sats
G Rewley Road
h Sunday nightsonly
j Arr. 4 38 aft.
^ Arr 5 54 mrn
k Arr. 9 35 aft. on Fris.
l Except 5 nm morns
P Arr 11 38 aft on Sats via Northampton (Castle)
R Arr 1 38 aft on Sats.
S or S Saturdays only
s Saturday night times
T Dep 10 55 mrn. on Sats.
t Thursdays only
TC Through Carriages
u Via Northampton (Castle)
U Arr. 8 26 aft. on Mons. and Fris.
V Via Northampton (Castle) on Sats
X 7 mins later on Sats.
Y Arr 12 44 aft on Sats
Z Arr 10 aft on Mons.
‡ Arr 1 2 aft on Sats
‡ Wednesdays and Saturdays

Table 3 — June 1951

BLETCHLEY, BANBURY AND OXFORD

Miles	Miles		WEEKDAYS					SX	SO										SUNDAYS	
			a.m.	a.m.	a.m.	a.m.	a.m.	a.m.	a.m.	p.m.	p.m.	p.m.	p.m.			p.m.	p.m.	p.m.	a.m.	a.m.
—	53	London (Euston)....dep.		6 40	7 35		10E50	12G 0	12 20	12 45	3 5			6 42	7 30				12 0	10 50
—	50	Liverpool (L. St.) ,,	12 10			8 20				9T15	11†40		4 10			4Z17		12 0	8 30	
—	50	Manchester (L. Rd.) ,,	12 0	12M35		88 5	8435	8K35	9T25	11†55		3b20			4Z35	12 0				
—	50	Birmingham (N. St.) ,,	12W020		7 30	8 45	10J30	10K30		2 30		5 23		7 40	12 20				10 35	
—	50	Rugby Midland .... ,,	3 40		8 24		9 50	12802	11K40	12V53	3 40		6 57		8 30	3 32			11 25	
—	50	Northampton (C.) ,,	4 18	6A55	8 0		10 23	12S051	1J42		4 15		7 12		9 3	4 5			11 56	
—	59	Cambridge .... ,,		7 37			9 30	11†18		2 5			6 15							9 50
0		Bletchley ....dep.	5 24	8 0	9 30		12 15	1 34	2 22	2 22	5 5	5 28		8 15	8 40	10 0		8 46		1 0
5		Swanbourne		8 10	9 40		12 25	1 44	2 32	2 32	5 15	5 38		8 25	8 50	1011		8 56		1 10
7		Winslow	5 40	7 40	8 17	9 46	12 30	1 49	2 37	2 37	5 22	5 44		8 30	8 56	1016		9 1		1 16
9		Verney Junction ...... arr.		7 44	8 22	9 51	12 35	1 54	2 42	2 42	5 27	5 49		8 35						
—	0	Verney Junction ...... dep.		8 25					2 43	2 43		5 50								
—	2	Padbury		8 29					2 47	2 47		5 54		9 5						
—	4	Buckingham ...... arr.		8 35					2 53	2 53		6 0		9 11						
		...... dep.		8 39					2 55	2 55		6 2								
—	9	Fulwell & Westbury		8 47					3 3	3 3		6 10								
—	12	Brackley		8 54					3 9	3 9		6 16								
—	17	Farthinghoe		9 5	9 57				3 20	3 20		6 27	7 18							
—	21	Banbury .... arr.		9 13	10 4				3 28	3 28		6 35	7 25							
—		Verney Junction ......dep.		7 45		9 52	12 37	1 55			5 28			8 36						
11		Claydon		7 48		9 55	1240	1 58			5 31			8 39		1024	9 9			1 24
15		Marsh Gibbon & Poundon ..		7 56		10 3	1248	2 6			5 40			8 48			9 18			1 33
17		Launton				10 7	1252	2 10			5 44			8 52			9 22			1 37
19		Bicester	6 3	8 9		10 13	12 57	2 16			5 50			8 58		1040	9 28			1 43
25		Islip	6 14	8 18		10 23	1 7	2 25			6 1			9 8			9 38			1 54
31		Oxford .... arr.	6 25	8 30		10 34	1 18	2 36			6 12			9 19		1056	9 49			2 5

† — a.m.
A — On Saturdays depart Northampton 7.10 a.m.
B — On Saturdays depart Manchester (L. Rd.) 8.10 a.m.
D — Calls at Launton on Wednesdays and Saturdays only.
E — On Saturdays dep. London (Euston) 10.55 a.m.
G — 12.0 noon and on Saturdays depart London (Euston) 12.5 p.m.
H — Arrive Northampton 7.11 p.m. and Rugby Midland 7.45 p.m. on Saturdays.
J — and is Saturdays only.
K — a.m., and is Wednesdays and Thursdays only.
L — Wednesdays and Thursdays only.
MO — Mondays only.
MX — Mondays excepted.
SO — Saturdays only.
SX — Saturdays excepted.
T — a.m., and commences June 30th.
V — Commences June 30th.
TC — Through Carriage.
Z — Via Birmingham.
b — Manchester (Mayfield).
d — On Saturdays arrive Northampton 12.41 p.m. Rugby Midland 12.41 p.m., Birmingham 2.6 p.m.
t — Arrive Northampton 8.11 a.m. and Rugby Midland 8.48 a.m. on Saturdays commencing June 30th.

June 1920   January 1944   June 1951

1. Oxford to Bletchley

OXFORD

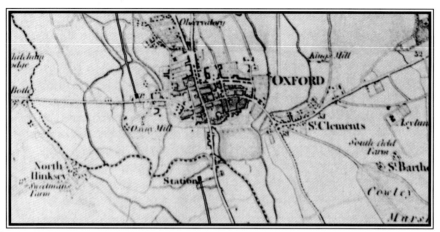

II.   A map from the late 1840s shows the GWR terminus south of Oxford and the proposed terminus of the branch from Bletchley west thereof. In the event, it was not completed until after the GWR's line north to Banbury was opened in 1850. The present through station did not open until 1st October 1852, trains having to reverse in and out of the old one. The terminus was used for goods until broad gauge was abandoned in 1872.

1.   An oval booking office was situated at the south end of the platforms, which were particularly low until about 1906. The nearest part of the building was used by the stationmaster.
(Lens of Sutton coll.)

III.   The 1921 edition at 6ins to 1 mile reveals the proximity of the two stations (lower left) and includes Port Meadow Halt (upper left), the platforms of which were on the LNWR route only.

2.   With the goods yard in the background, the outer end of the platform was recorded in 1904 with 2-2-2 no. 622 *Prince Alfred*. The leading wheels have splash guards. (R.S.Carpenter coll.)

3.   The original roof had been of a modular design as used for the Crystal Pawlace and was erected by the same builder. The 1888 replacement is seen in 1914, together with 2-4-2T no. 413 (later LMS no. 6660), which lasted until 1947. (C.G.Maggs coll.)

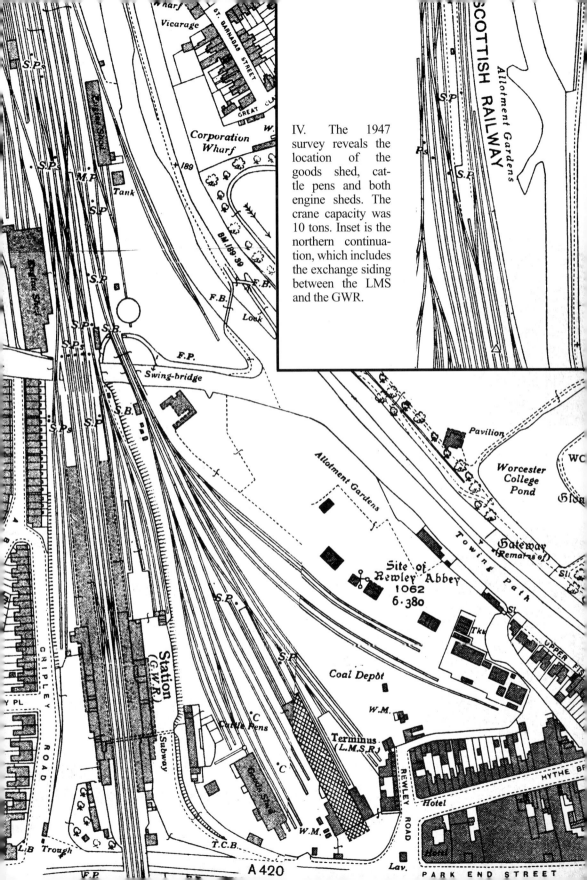

IV. The 1947 survey reveals the location of the goods shed, cattle pens and both engine sheds. The crane capacity was 10 tons. Inset is the northern continuation, which includes the exchange siding between the LMS and the GWR.

Wharf
Vicarage
ST. BARNABAS STREET
GREAT CL
Corporation Wharf
+ 189
BM 189·99
F.B.
F.B.
Lock
S.P.
M.P.
Tank
S.P.
S.P.
S.P.
S.P.
S.P.
S.B.
Engine Shed
Engine Shed
F.P.
Swing-bridge
S.B.
S.P.
S.P.

SCOTTISH RAILWAY
Allotment Gardens
S.P.
P.
S.P.
S.P.

Pavilion
Worcester College Pond
Allotment Gardens
Towing Path
Gateway (Remains of)
Site of Rewley Abbey
1062
6·380
Tkt
UPPER

Station (G.W.R.)
S.P.
S.P.
S.P.
Coal Depot
W.M.
CRIPLEY ROAD
PL
Subway
Cattle Pens
·C
·C
Terminus (L.M.S.R.)
Goods Sd
W.M.
Hotel
REWLEY ROAD
HYTHE BR
L.B. Trough
F.P.
T.C.B.
W.M.
Hotel
Lav.
A 420
PARK END STREET

4.   A 1919 panorama includes about half of the sidings. The majority of Oxford's domestic coal arrived in this goods yard, known as "Rewley Road". This name did not appear in timetables (except Bradshaw's) nor on sign boards. (NRM)

5.   The three-car articulated diesel unit was replaced by a 2-6-4T with two coaches during periods of withdrawal or failure. The locomotive had difficulty in maintaining the schedule, which was only in force for a few months. (Lens of Sutton coll.)

ADDITIONAL EXPERIMENTAL EXPRESS SERVICES

By DIESEL TRAIN

(1st and 3rd Class)

BETWEEN

OXFORD, BLETCHLEY, BEDFORD and CAMBRIDGE

EACH WEEKDAY commencing SEPT. 12th
1938

(subject to cancellation without notice)

				a.m.	SX p.m.	SO p.m.	p.m.	SX p.m.	SO p.m.
OXFORD ...	...	...	dep.	...	1 40	1 46	6 25	10 45	11 10
Islip ...	...	...	dep.	...	...	...	...	...	11 18
Bicester...	...	...	dep.	...	...	...	...	10 59	11 27
Winslow	...	...	dep.	...	...	...	...	11 15	11 43
BLETCHLEY	...	...	arr.	...	2 18	2 23	7 9	11 24	11 52
			dep	8 45	2 25	2 25	7 12		
BEDFORD (St. John's)..			arr.	9 6	2 44	2 44	7 32		
			dep.	9 7	2 45	2 45	7 34		
SANDY ...	...	...	arr.	9 24	3 5	3 5	7 50		
			dep.	9 25	3 6	3 6	7 51		
CAMBRIDGE	...	...	arr.	9 51	3 32	3 32	8 17		

				a.m.	p.m.	p.m.
CAMBRIDGE	...	...	dep.	10 42	4 15	8 40
SANDY ...	...	...	arr.	11 8	4 41	9 5
			dep.	11 9	4 42	9 6
BEDFORD (St. John's)...			arr.	11 27	4 59	9 24
			dep.	11 28	5 0	9 27
BLETCHLEY	...	...	arr.	11 49	5 21	9 48
			dep.	11 50	5 24	10 5
OXFORD ...	...	...	arr.	p.m. 12 28	6 2	10 43

SX—Saturdays excepted   SO—Saturdays only

EXISTING CHEAP FACILITIES ARE AVAILABLE BY THESE SERVICES

Further information may be obtained on application to the L M S Stations, or to Mr. H. HAUXWELL, District Goods and Passenger Manager, Castle Station, Northampton ; or Mr. D. S. INMAN, District Goods and Passenger Manager, Leicester

September 1938   T. E. ARGILE, Acting Chief Commercial Manager

V.   This information appeared only on handbills and not in timetable books. Note the high speeds and few stops.

6.   The LMS certainly made its presence felt in Oxford in the 1930s. The outer components remained from the original cast iron modular construction. (R.M.Casserley coll.)

7.   The 5.0pm departure for Bedford was hauled by 4-4-0 no. 551 on 11th February 1948. Note that trains could depart from either platform. All trains arrived on the left. (H.C.Casserley)

8.   Passenger trains ceased to use the station on 1st October 1951 and were transferred to the ex-GWR one, mostly using the bay platforms. This is the scene on 2nd June 1956. (R.M.Casserley)

9.   This panorama from about 1962 includes the former LNWR goods shed. The tall building beyond the station roof was occupied by Frank Cooper, Oxford's famous marmalade producer. The yard was in use until 5th April 1984 and is now covered with houses. (Lens of Sutton coll.)

10.   Comparison with picture 6 will show that one roof span was removed. The building was used as a hostel for railwaymen and later as an exhaust and tyre centre. Only the end span was original. (Lens of Sutton coll.)

11.   Although long listed Grade II, Oxford lost the station used by passengers for 100 years. It is seen on 14th December 1998 as dismantling began. It was rebuilt next year at the Buckinghamshire Railway Centre, close to Quainton Road station. (M.J.Stretton)

12.   The introduction of a local service to Bicester meant that two trains had to use the up bay platform simultaneously. The 17.43 is spurned by passengers on 22nd July 1993 who rush by to catch the 17.33 to Moreton-in-Marsh. (M.J.Stretton)

13.   Having arrived at platform 3 on 5th September 1996 is the 18.09 from Bicester Town, operated by Thames Trains. First Great Western Link provided the service from 1st April 2004. (M.J.Stretton)

14.   Immediately after leaving the station, trains passed over the swing bridge spanning Sheepwash Channel, which connected the canal with the river via a lock. No. 25845 is on the bridge on 6th July 1946, followed by no. 25694, both "Prince of Wales" class 4-6-0s. The lattice structure on the right carries the point rodding high above the water, while the vertical posts above it bear the pulleys for the signal wires. (E.Johnson)

15.   On the left is the ex-LNWR 36-lever signal box, which was in use until 31st July 1959. In line with the back of the former GWR box is the rodding bridge described in caption 14. (M.J.Stretton coll.)

16.   The 73ft long bridge weighed 85 tons and was cranked manually by two men through gearing. Records show that it was opened about six times daily in 1907. All shunting movements involved crossing it. On the left is the ground frame which replaced the signal box and was in use until 2nd May 1978. (I.Nash)

17.   Another view from December 1975 includes North Box, which had closed in 1973. The up bay is also visible. (I.Nash)

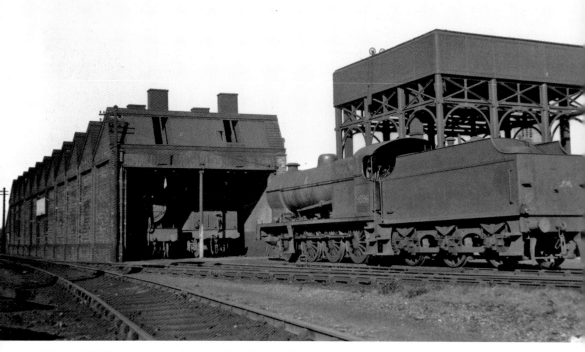

18.	Initially there was a three-road engine shed with timber framing which housed nine engines. It was replaced by this solid structure in 1883; it accommodated six locomotives. Class 7F no. 9596 was recorded on 24th October 1937. (A.N.H.Glover/F.A.Wycherley)

19.	The 42ft turntable was replaced by a 50ft one in 1928. Ex-LNWR "19ins Goods" 4-6-0 no. 8701 is on it in the late 1930s. Two sidings were provided on the left for exchange traffic with the Oxford Canal. (Lens of Sutton coll.)

20.   The shed was closed on 3rd December 1950, as there were extensive ex-GWR facilities on the other side of the main lines. The coal stage had belatedly received a roof in March 1950. The photo is from May 1958; demolition took place in 1962. (R.M.Casserley)

> **Other pictures of the area can be found in**
> ***Branch Lines around Princes Risborough,***
> ***Branch Line to Fairford, Didcot to Banbury* and**
> ***Oxford to Moreton-in-Marsh.***

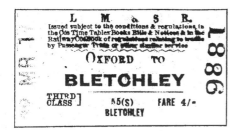

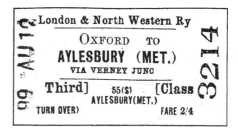

21.　　This and picture 22 feature a non-navigable link between the canal and the river. Seen from Walton Well Road Bridge on 26th February 1958 are the former LNWR lines on the left, the connection to the GWR route on the left and ex-GWR 2-6-0 no. 5397 waiting with an up goods train. The link lines were in use from 1st November 1940 until 29th October 1973, as was Oxford North Junction box, out of view on the left. (R.M.Casserley)

Inset - Oxford North Junction box was photographed on 12th September 1963; it had 88 levers. Most wartime boxes had flat roofs. (R.Webster)

(right) 22. From almost the same view point, we witness Cambridge-based ex-LNER class D16/3 4-4-0 no. 62571 accelerating a Bletchley stopping train on 19th March 1952, while another up freight waits at the signals. Until 1940, there was an indirect exchange siding for 22 wagons between the two companies' tracks. It was used regularly by mail vans between Glasgow and Southampton, but the connections were on a gradient of 1 in 30. (A.Ford/ M.J.Stretton)

(right) 23. We look north on 14th April 1962 as yet another up goods (left) stands at signals. It is waiting for ex-LMS 4-6-0 no. 45037 to cross in front of it with a parcels train from Bletchley. The junction for the single line to Bicester was moved about half a mile north in 1973. The tracks on the right were abandoned. (M.A.N.Johnston)

PORT MEADOW HALT

24.   Map III indicates the location of this northward view of "Precedent" class 2-4-0 no. 1170. On the right is the halt, which was named "Summertown" until January 1907. It was open from 9th October 1905 to 1st January 1917 and from 5th May 1919 to 30th October 1926, although the last train was on the 25th due to the General Strike. (R.M.Casserley coll.)

25.   From the same footbridge, we witness class 4F 0-6-0 no. 3920 and see the same occupation crossing on 11th March 1946. The halt had long gone and goods loops had been opened on 14th December 1941 and closed on 28th August 1960, along with the signal box, in the distance. (H.C.Casserley)

26.   A northward view from the crossing shows the up goods loop more clearly. "Up" is to London, but was in opposite directions on the two railways at this location. Class G1 0-8-0 no. 9297 is working a special train for the War Department on 6th May 1942. It was probably from Bicester Camp. (A.W.V.Mace/Milepost 92½)

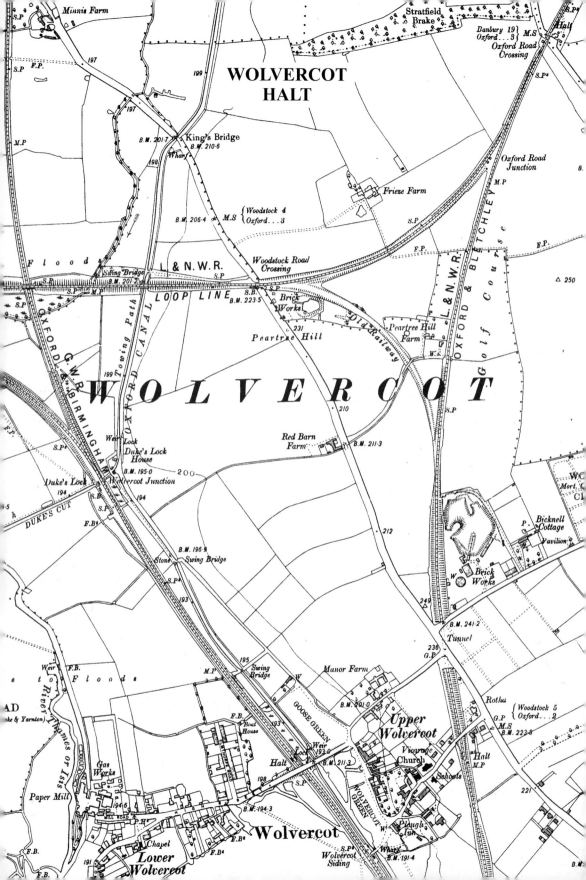

(left) VI. The 1914 survey at 6ins to 1 mile has our route close to the right border and the halt near the church at Upper Wolvercot. The GWR's main line is annotated and its route to Moreton-in-Marsh and Worcester curves to the left border. This was built by the Oxford, Worcester & Wolverhampton Railway to mixed gauge, but the broad gauge was never used regularly. The passenger trains mostly ran into the GWR station at Oxford, that company operating the route from 1863. Goods traffic was routed to Oxford's LNWR station via the curve marked *Old Railway*. The connection marked LOOP LINE opened in April 1854 and carried a Euston service via a curve at Bletchley until September 1861. The loop was an important freight route, particularly during World War II. It was operated with "Permissive Working", whereby around six goods trains each way could use it simultaneously, drivers using their eyes instead of signals. It was also used for ironstone from the Midlands to South Wales. The tunnel north of the halt is 140yds in length and is now beneath the Woodstock Road roundabout.

27. The platform is just visible to the left of the LNWR steam railmotor. This type was in use from 1905 to about 1921. The opening dates are as in caption 24. The same applies to Oxford Road Halt, near the top edge of map VII. (Lens of Sutton coll.)

28. Oxford Road Junction is top right on map VI; note that the tracks run parallel for some distance. This is looking towards Oxford in 1929. The lines on the right were taken out of use on 8th November

1965, the level crossing having been replaced by a bridge in 1935. There was a siding behind the camera, this serving a grain silo (erected in WWII) until 1967. Part of the siding was used as an Amey stone terminal from 1973. (Mowat coll./ Brunel Uni.)

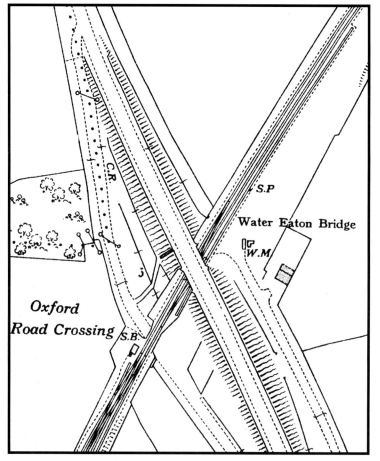

VII. The 1936 edition has the siding in full and includes the weighing machine of the small yard, which was renamed Banbury Road Sidings in May 1964. Goods traffic ceased on 1st January 1974. The area here had been used as a temporary terminus for the line from Bletchley; at least one excursion train was recorded.

29. A new signal box was opened on 4th November 1956 and was immediately to the east of the old one. It was renamed on 15th September 1958 "Banbury Road Junction" to avoid confusion with a site near Reading. Closure came on 29th October 1973. The photo is from October 1969. (R. Webster)

ISLIP

VIII. The 1922 survey reveals the proximity of the station to the centre of the village. W.M. refers to a weighing machine. The population rose slightly from 554 in 1901 to 620 in 1961.

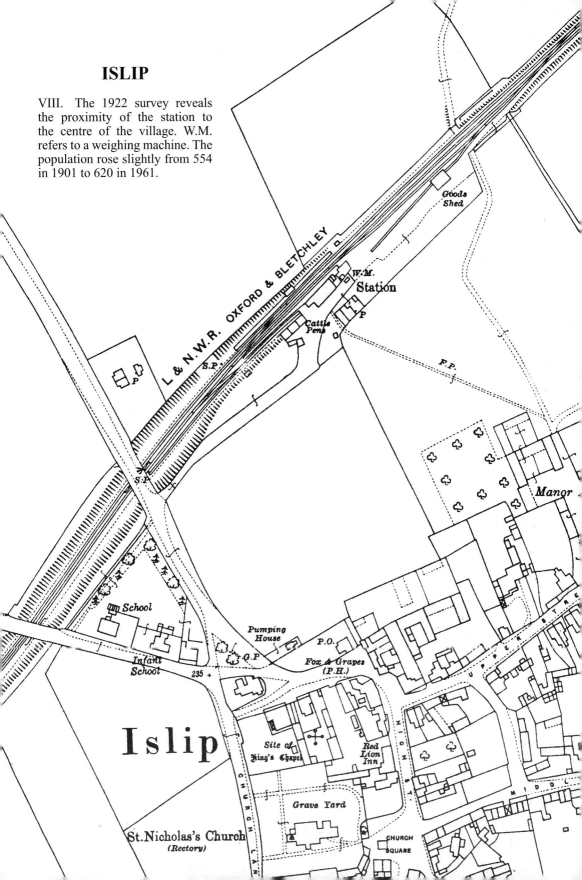

Goods Shed

L & N.W.R. OXFORD & BLETCHLEY

W.M.
Station

Cattle Pens

S.P.

P

P

S.P.

F.P.

Manor

School

Pumping House

P.O.

G.P.

Fox & Grapes (P.H.)

Infant School

235 +

UPPER STREET

Islip

Site of King's Chapel

Red Lion Inn

HIGH ST.

MIDDLE

CHURCH LANE

Grave Yard

CHURCH SQUARE

St. Nicholas's Church
(Rectory)

30.   The inclined station approach is evident in this 1900 view, as is a double-armed signal post. Milk traffic was heavy and a train from Bletchley terminated here on Sundays to collect it. (LGRP)

31.   A 1933 view towards Bicester includes the goods shed which was in use until 7th September 1964. Oil lighting was universal here. The station was particularly busy for three days each year prior to WWII, when many horses, riders and spectators arrived for Oddington Races. (Mowat coll./Brunel University)

32.   The frames on the left of this 1961 photo were associated with an Esso oil distribution depot, which was served by two sidings. It had been established by the Air Ministry prior to the war and was in use until at least 1974. The cattle dock is on the right. (Stations UK)

33.   For many years the signalling instruments were in the booking office, but they were moved in 1956 onto the wall on the left to be close to the seven-lever ground frame, which is just out of the picture. There was another two-lever frame for the oil siding. (Lens of Sutton coll.)

34.   Following the experimental reopening of the line to Bicester Town in 1987, a new platform was built and it was opened on 15th January 1989. The 13.51 from Bicester Town was recorded on 21st April 1995, formed of Thames Turbo no. 165121. (C.G.Maggs)

35.   The boiler end of a steam railmotor is clear, unlike the platform, which is probably that at Oddington, 1½ miles from Islip. (Lens of Sutton coll.)

L. & N.W.R.—To and from Oxford and Bicester.
WEEK DAYS ONLY.

UP. Stations.	M		M				M	S		M					M		M		M	T
	a m	a m	a m	a m	a m	a m	n'n	p m	p m	p m	p m	p m	p m	p m	p m	p m	p m	p m	p m	p m
OXFORD dep	7 15	7 45	9 3	9 45	1050	1125	12 0	1230	1255	1 50	2 25	4 40	4 50	5 40	6 50	7 25	11 0			
Port Meadow	7 17	..	9 5	..	..	1127	..	..	..	1 52	..	..	4 52	..	6 52	..	11 2			
Wolvercote	7 21	..	9 9	..	..	1131	..	..	..	1 56	..	..	4 56	..	6 56	..	11 6			
Oxford Road	7 25	..	9 13	..	..	1135	..	..	..	2 0	..	..	5 0	..	7 0	..	1110			
Islip ..	7 32	7 57	9 20	9 57	..	1142	121?	1242	..	2 7	2 37	4 51	5 7	..	7 7	7 37	1116			
Oddington	7 37	..	9 24	..	..	1146	..	..	..	2 11	..	..	5 11	..	7 11	..	..			
Charlton..	7 41	..	9 29	..	..	1151	..	..	..	2 16	..	..	5 16	..	7 16	..	1124			
Wendlebury	7 47	..	9 35	..	..	1157	..	..	..	2 22	..	..	5 22	..	7 22	..	..			
BICESTER ar	7 50	8 7	9 40	10 7	11 7	12 2	1222	1255	1 12	2 27	2 49	5	1 5	27	5 56	7 27	7 48	1132		

DOWN Stations.	M		M				M	S		M				M		M		M	T
	a m	a m	a m	a m	a m	p m	p m	p m	p m	p m	p m	p m	p m	p m	p m	p m	p m	p m	p m
BICESTER dp	8 0	9 13	9 50	11 2	1152	1220	1 15	2 55	3 15	4 9	5 6	5 35	7 45	8 10	9 37	..	1140		
Wendlebury	8 4	..	9 55	..	..	1225	..	..	3 20	..	..	5 40	..	8 15	..	..	..		
Charlton ..	8 9	..	10 1	..	..	1231	..	..	3 26	..	..	5 46	..	8 21	..	..	..		
Oddington	8 13	..	10 6	..	..	1236	..	..	3 31	..	..	5 51	..	8 26	..	..	..		
Islip.. ..	8 17	9 25	10 10	1114	..	1240	1 28	3	8 3 35	..	5 18	5 55	7 57	8 30	a	..	..		
Oxford Road	8 23	..	1017	..	..	1247	..	..	3 42	..	..	6 2	..	8 37	..	..	..		
Wolvercote	8 25	..	1021	..	..	1251	..	..	3 46	..	..	6 6	..	8 41	..	..	..		
Port Meadow	8 28	..	1024	..	..	1254	..	..	3 49	..	..	6 9	..	8 44	..	..	..		
OXFORD arr	8 30	9 35	1027	1125	1210	1257	1 42	3 20	3 52	4 27	5 30	6 12	8 10	8 47	10 0	..	12 5		

s—Sats. only.   M—Rail Motor Car—One Class only.   T—Thurs. and Sats. only.

a Calls if required on notice.

October 1905

36.   The site of Oddington Halt was recorded in 1958, looking towards Bicester. The stylish cottage was of Buckinghamshire Railway origin. The gates here and at Wendlebury were replaced by automatic open crossings, when the line was singled on 29th October 1973. (R.M.Casserley)

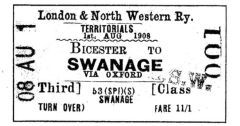

London & North Western Ry.
TERRITORIALS
1st AUG 1908
BICESTER   TO
SWANAGE
VIA OXFORD
Third] 53(SPI)(S) [Class
                SWANAGE
TURN OVER)   FARE 11/1

London & North Western Ry
Issued subject to the conditions & regulations in
the Cos Time Tables Books Bills & Notices.
BICESTER   TO
WINSLOW
Third] 53(S) [Class
            WINSLOW   FARE 1/0½

37.   Charlton Halt was on level straight track, almost four miles from Islip. This northward view of the site is from 1958 and is typical of the route. (R.M.Casserley)

38.   Wendlebury Halt had been built close to a Roman station. It was at Langford Lane crossing, over one mile from Bicester. We are looking towards that station in February 1957. The dates for these halts are as in caption 24. (R.M.Casserley)

BICESTER MILITARY RAILWAY

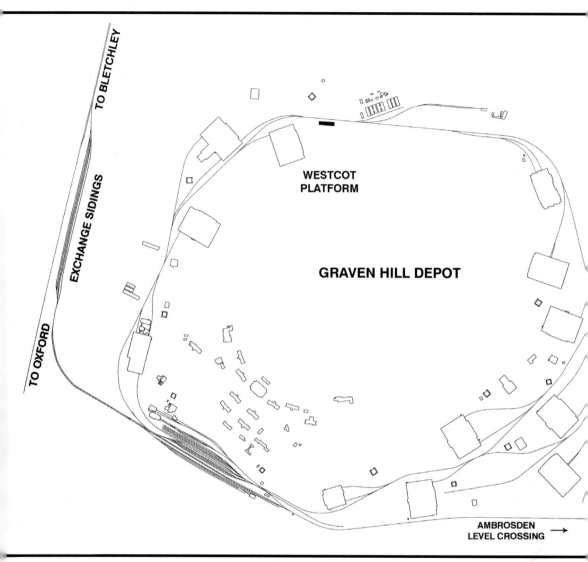

IX.   Bicester No. 2 box was opened on 9th November 1941 to give access to the five exchange sidings; by the end of the war there were over 70 miles of track handling up to 400 wagons per day and over 30,000 passengers per week, trains being run direct to Oxford daily. The railway, though operating on a much smaller scale than when it opened in WWII, is currently operated by Defence Rail & Container Services, part of the MOD's Defence, Storage & Distribution Agency. The railway dates back to 1942 when two hills near the villages of Ambrosden and Arncott in rural Oxfordshire were selected by the War Department as the sites for two major ordnance depots. Numerous storage sheds were built around the two hills and they were laid out in such a way as to make enemy bombing extremely difficult. From the start, the depots were rail served, each site having an extensive circular main line with numerous spurs serving the storage sheds, as well as a 2½ mile line between the two sites. The Ambrosden site, more often referred to as Graven Hill, includes the extensive exchange sidings and ¼ mile further on into the depot are the sorting sidings, which to this day serve both sites and are to be found next to the locomotive depot. Both of the circuits were always operated counter-clockwise with wagons being propelled into the sheds. There are also regulating sidings at Arncott where trains wait until they are called forward to go round the circuit to serve the sheds, though much of the Arncott site has been abandoned in recent years. The Graven Hill circuit does however still operate in its entirety.   The 30-lever Bicester No. 2 box was replaced by a ground frame on 29th October 1973. Piddington (beyond the right border) received a regular passenger service from Oxford for many years.

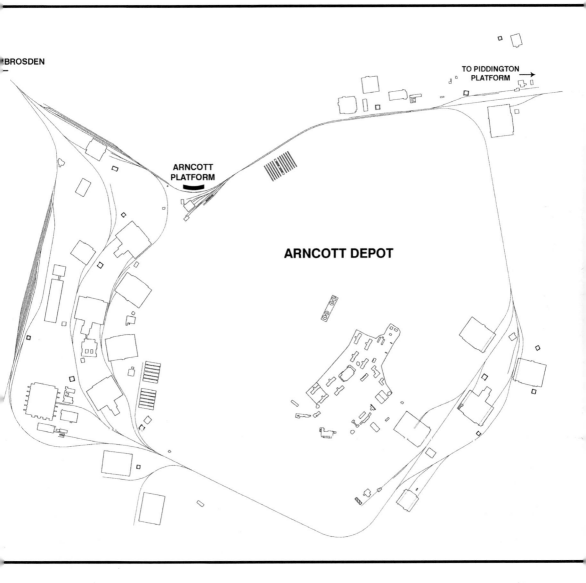

BROSDEN

TO PIDDINGTON
PLATFORM

ARNCOTT
PLATFORM

ARNCOTT DEPOT

39.　　There were often ten locomotives in use simultaneously, this example being an ex-GWR Dean Goods, showing the WD number 70095 on 23rd April 1946. (E.Johnson)

40.　　Seen on the same day at the coal dock is WD no. 75111, a more modern Hunslet Austerity 0-6-0ST from the Ministry of Supply. (E.Johnson)

41.   Ambrosden Platform is seen after it had ceased to be used in the 1960s. Dean Goods 0-6-0s had earlier run regular services to Oxford from here. The structure has long gone; trains to Oxford ceased in the late 1960s. (DRCS)

42.   We look west from a diesel as it approaches Graven Hill "A" Block Post on 31st May 1995. A civilian signalman is waiting to collect the single line tablet. (C.G.Maggs)

43. This view is of White Cross Green level crossing, which is in the southern part of the Arncott Depot and is seen in 2002. The gates appear to be of GWR origin. (C.Morgan)

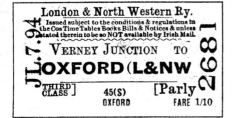

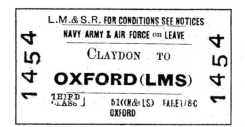

44. We look southwards from the back of a locomotive hauling a train of Warflats. Its rear is near Arncott "B" Cabin. EWS trains depart most days for Didcot, where they are remarshalled for destinations such as Shoeburyness, Cardiff, Marchwood, Glen Douglas and sometimes mainland Europe. (DRCS)

45. This is a view of the sorting sidings from a point outside the main office. The line on the right served the boiler house until 2002, the year in which the photo was taken. (C.Morgan)

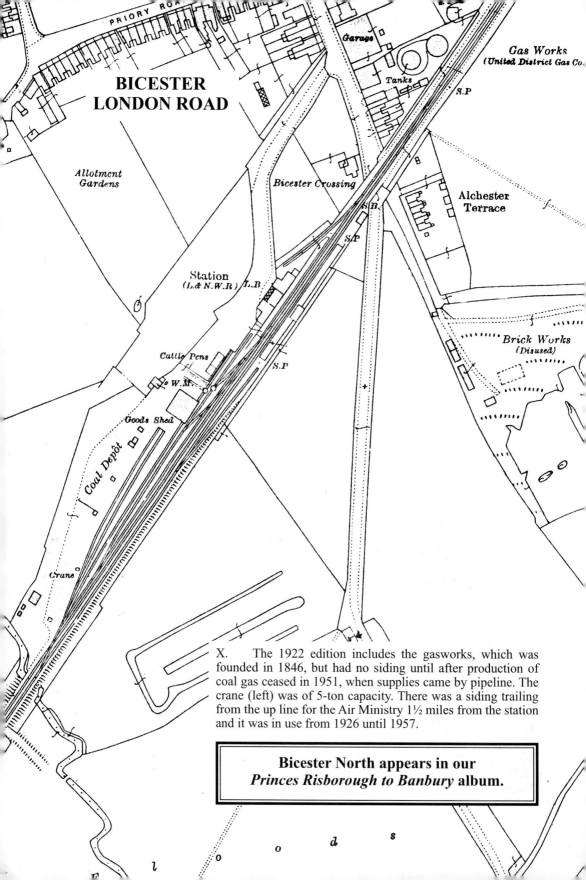

PRIORY RO

**BICESTER
LONDON ROAD**

Garage

Gas Works
(United District Gas Co.)

Tanks

S.P

Allotment
Gardens

Bicester Crossing

Alchester
Terrace

S.B

S.P

Station
(L.& N.W.R.) L.B.

Cattle Pens

S.P

W.M.

Goods Shed

Brick Works
(Disused)

Coal Depôt

Crane

X.   The 1922 edition includes the gasworks, which was
founded in 1846, but had no siding until after production of
coal gas ceased in 1951, when supplies came by pipeline. The
crane (left) was of 5-ton capacity. There was a siding trailing
from the up line for the Air Ministry 1½ miles from the station
and it was in use from 1926 until 1957.

**Bicester North appears in our
Princes Risborough to Banbury album.**

46.   A northward panorama has the station house centre. The main building was constructed of limestone blocks, while the shelter on the down platform was timber clad. (Lens of Sutton coll.)

47.   The guard has his hand at the top of a handrail which would be swung out, together with three steps, at halts with low platforms. The mechanism was linked to the vacuum brakes for safety. The car seated 48. (R.S.Carpenter coll.)

48.   The goods shed was also of wooden construction, a technique used widely by the LNWR. Under the water tank is the usual coal store; the next door leads to the lamp room and beyond that is the porters room in this 1933 photo. (Mowat coll./Brunel University)

49.   An unusual viewpoint was adopted for this 1950s photograph, which features the gents, beyond which is the stationmasters office. (LGRP)

50.   The suffix "London Road" was added to the nameboard on 20th September 1954. No. 80039 was in disgusting condition when working the 4.45pm Oxford to Bletchley train on 3rd June 1956. (T.J.Edgington)

51.   The crossing gates were replaced by lifting barriers in 1976. This February 1957 northward panorama shows the proximity of the gas holder to the track. The signal box was termed Bicester No. 1 from 9th November 1941 and was closed on 24th May 1986. It had 26 levers. (R.M.Casserley)

52.   This is the view from the signal box in 1967; the signalman had to keep the foot crossing under careful observation. There was only one other station on the route with a footbridge. (E.Wilmshurst)

53.   An Oxford-bound train arrives on 30th December 1967. Passenger numbers had diminished, although the population had risen from 3000 in 1901 to almost 7000 in 1961. (E.Wilmshurst)

BICESTER TOWN

54.   This photograph is from 26th April 1989. The station was unstaffed and tickets were issued on the train. The line northward had been singled in 1986, but the track on the right was used as a headshunt. The approach to the station had been ruined by a coach store, but worse was to come. Destruction of one of the most important buildings in the town's history was permitted. It was by then in private ownership. (D.A.Thompson)

55.   The result of authorised vandalism was to be seen on 21st April 1995, as no. 165121 was about to depart for Oxford at 15.54. (C.G.Maggs)

56. Demand for gas rose above the pipeline capacity and so a new works opened in April 1968 and two sidings were laid down further north for the reception of naphtha, crude petrol. Gas ceased to be made from this in June 1971, but the last train ran on 13th June 1969. The naphtha storage tanks are on the left; the spheres in the background are for propane. The loco is a 1958 Fowler, which had been at Camberley and later went to Reading. (Southern Gas)

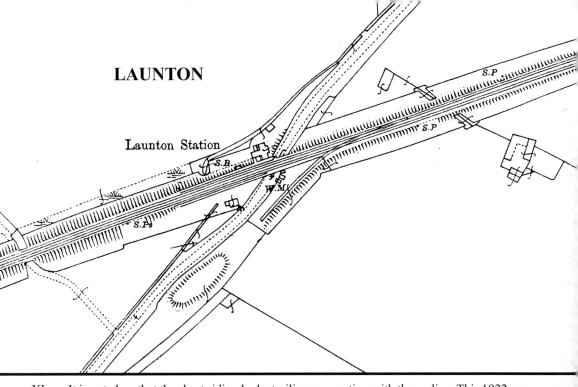

LAUNTON

Launton Station

XI.   It is not clear that the short siding had a trailing connection with the up line. This 1922 map includes a weighing machine.

57.   A foot crossing and oil lamps served to the end. Being over one mile from the village, the expense of providing mains water and electricity was considered too great. The ground frame was to the right of the white posts and the block instruments were in the booking office. One point rod passes under the boards. (Stations UK)

58.   Low platforms remained until closure, as seen in another 1961 photograph. Back in 1883, the service offered was an up train at 9.10am and down ones at 8.19am and 8.2pm. It improved later, although there were only 545 inhabitants recorded in 1901. Standing outside the ladies room is a set of steps for use by less agile passengers. The house appeared to be single storey from platform level, but as the line was on an embankment the entrance was lower. (Lens of Sutton coll.)

59.   This is a 1971 view of the house from the site of the goods siding, which had closed on 30th November 1959. The building became a private residence after an automatic open crossing was installed in 1976. (R.M.Casserley)

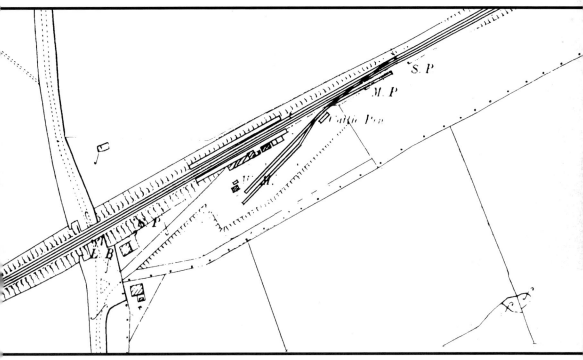

XII.   This station opened later than the others on 7th August 1880. The 1886 edition shows an arrangement which never changed, apart from the addition of a building on the up platform.

60.   As at Launton, the goods connection trailed from the up line, but here it divided into two sidings. This is a 1933 view and includes a lower quadrant signal, which would soon be replaced. (LGRP)

61.   A photograph from 16th June 1958 reveals that the up platform shelter was of the old weather forecasters pattern. Car parking at one shilling was expensive; Mr. Casserley's Hillman Minx was in transit on a photographic mission for which we are all grateful. (H.C.Casserley)

62.   Goods traffic ceased here on 2nd November 1964. The station was one mile north of Marsh Gibbon and almost as far south of Poundon in slightly undulating countryside, which is evident here. The platforms had been raised in 1906; the evidence can be seen. The bay window is around the 12-lever frame and associated block instruments in this picture from about 1962. The box closed in January 1965. (Lens of Sutton coll.)

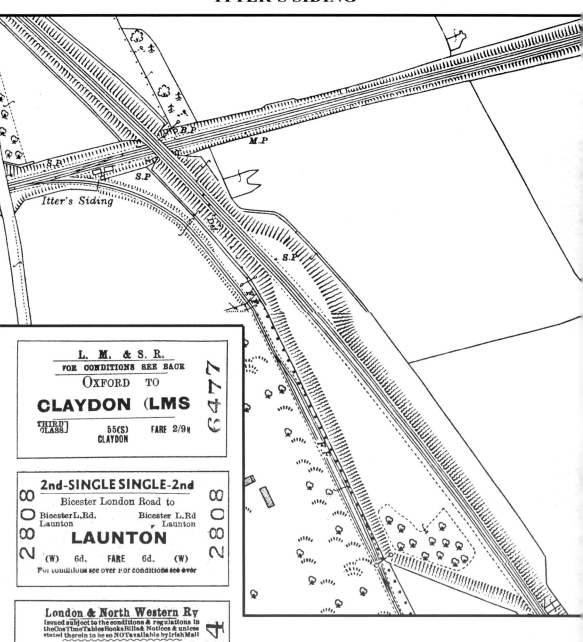

Itter's Siding

L. M. & S. R.
FOR CONDITIONS SEE BACK
OXFORD TO
CLAYDON (LMS
THIRD CLASS] 55(S) FARE 2/9
CLAYDON
6477

2nd-SINGLE SINGLE-2nd
Bicester London Road to
Bicester L.Rd. Bicester L.Rd
Launton Launton
LAUNTON
(W) 6d. FARE 6d. (W)
For conditions see over For conditions see over
2808 2808

London & North Western Ry
Issued subject to the conditions & regulations in
theCos Time Tables Books Bills & Notices & unless
stated therein to be so NOT available by Irish Mail
CLAYDON TO
WINSLOW
THIRD CLASS] 51(S.) [Parly
WINSLOW FARE -/4
6114

XIII.   The GCR built a bridge over the LNWR to carry its 1898 Midland main line from London. A siding had been laid nearby to Itter's Brickworks, which was one mile to the south, near the GCR's Calvert station.

63.   Two photographs from the road bridge on 15th May 1939 have the LNER main line in the background. "Prince of Wales" class 4-6-0 no. 25845 speeds west; it was the only member of the class to be completed by the LMS and was exhibited at the British Empire Exhibition at Wembley. (H.C.Casserley)

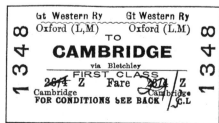

64.   Having left its train on the down line, class G2 0-8-0 shunts the siding. Out of sight, beyond the embankment, was Claydon L&NE Junction box, on the up side. The siding was used by the London Brick Company from its takeover in 1933 until 6th December 1977. (H.C.Casserley)

65.   This is a westward view from Claydon L&NE box, which was built with 26 levers during World War II to control a double track spur to the LNER line. It did not carry a regular passenger service and was reduced to a single line later. The box was closed on 30th September 1985 and a panel was brought into use in a Portacabin on the south side of the track. Colour light signals were installed and the route was used by DMUs, based at Aylesbury, to reach Bletchley TMD for servicing. These movements ceased on 14th May 1991 and the line eastwards was mothballed. It was grass covered in 2005. (British Railways)

CLAYDON

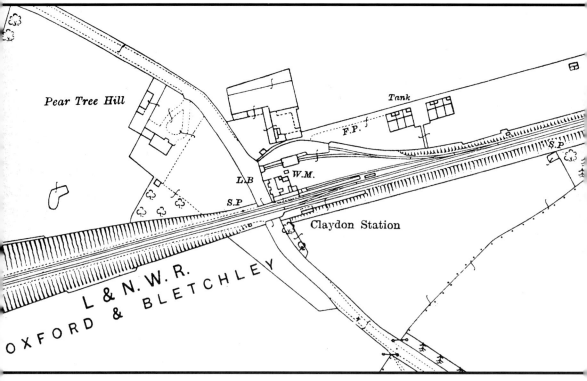

Pear Tree Hill

Tank

F.P.

L.B   W.M.

S.P

S.P.

Claydon Station

L & N.W.R.
OXFORD & BLETCHLEY

XIV.   The 1923 survey marks the position of some of the six signals. There was an eight-lever ground frame near the level crossing.

66.   Typical Buckinghamshire Railway architecture is seen again, along with an LNWR signal in about 1921. The granite wagon was probably bringing stone for local road improvements at that time. (Lens of Sutton coll.)

67.   A separate gate-keepers hut and more generous weather protection were provided here than elsewhere on the route. A DMU bound for Cambridge approaches in 1961. (Stations UK)

68.   Featured in detail are the architectural refinements and evidence of the not-uncommon enthusiasm of the staff for horticulture. One wagon is in the goods yard; it closed on 6th January 1964. The gates were replaced by an automatic open crossing in 1976. Oil lamps are seen around 1962. More than half a mile to the north was Steeple Claydon and the smaller Middle Claydon was to the south, as were two other Claydons with a total population of 686 in 1961.
(Lens of Sutton coll.)

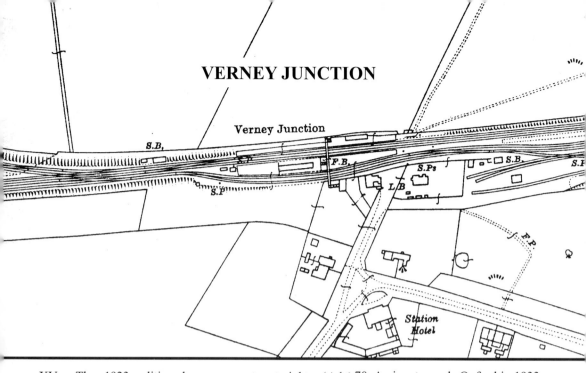

VERNEY JUNCTION

Verney Junction

S.B.

F.B.

S.Ps

S.B.

S.P

L.B.

S.P.

F.P.

Station Hotel

XV. The 1923 edition has our route straight across, with the Banbury branch curving on the left and the tracks to Quainton Road on the right, lower. They were opened by the Aylesbury & Buckingham Railway in 1868 and the GWR operated its service until 1891.

69. A horse box is coupled next to 2-4-2T no. 323, bound for Bletchley in the early years of the 20th century. The station opened on 23rd September 1868 as a junction intended for use by the Metropolitan Railway. Sir Harry Verney was chairman of the Buckinghamshire Railway. He lived in nearby Claydon House. Calvert station (GCR) was named after the previous occupants, although opened later. (Lens of Sutton coll.)

(right) 70. A view towards Oxford in 1933 includes the single connection with the Met and the Banbury lines curving right beyond the signal box, which closed on 9th July 1967. The Banbury route was single from near the right border of the picture. (Mowat coll./Brunel University)

(lower right) 71. A Metropolitan Railway train stands on the right. These trains terminated here from 1st July 1891 until 6th July 1936; Pullman cars were operated in 1910-14. Ex-LNWR 0-6-0 no. 8367 runs in with the 5.27pm Bletchley to Banbury train on 2nd May 1936. (H.C.Casserley)

72.   A few minutes later, the locomotive of the Met train has run round and backed on. It is 4-4-4T no. 107 and it will depart for Baker Street at 6.20pm. It was soon to be purchased by the LNER. Also visible is the former Met signal box, together with a perforated signal post. London Transport had taken over the Met in 1933 and cut back its operation to Aylesbury within three years. The exchange sidings are beyond the signal box. (H.C.Casserley)

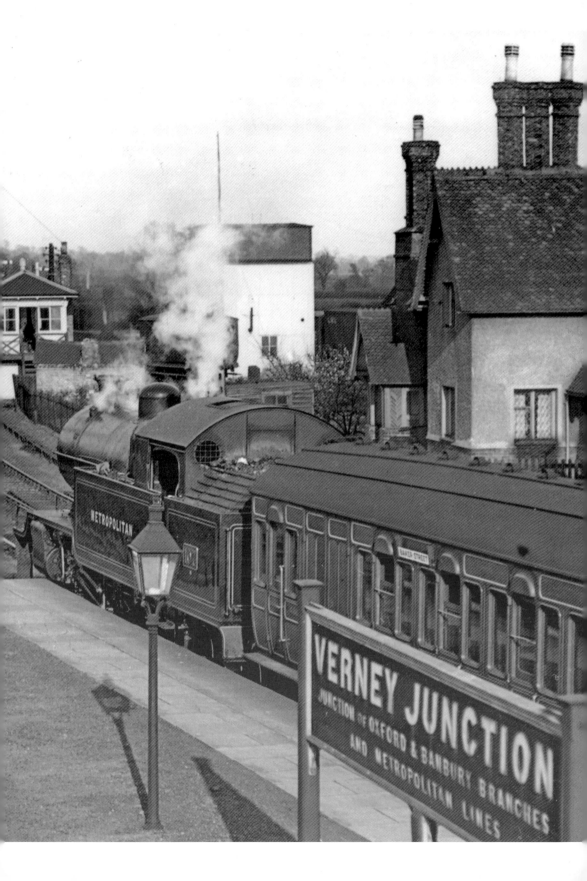

METROPOLITAN

BAKER STREET

VERNEY JUNCTION
JUNCTION OF OXFORD & BANBURY BRANCHES
AND METROPOLITAN LINES

73.	The 11.52am from Oxford was hauled by 4-4-0 no. 1155 on 11th September 1937, while the autotrain to Buckingham was worked by class 2P no. 6699. It would soon pass behind the signal box. The unusual coach was formerly a petrol-electric railcar. (H.C.Casserley)

74.	By 1955, few passengers changed here and had time to enjoy the goldfish, a model windmill, an immobile heron and posed mermaids amongst other joys of a more leisurely age. (H.C.Casserley)

75.   Until 1891, the ladies room had been in the station house (right), while the urinal was on the up platform (left). The former Met lines continued to carry some freight traffic, particularly during WWII. These were eventually lifted in 1957, except for some track used for carriage and wagon storage. This Bletchley-bound train was photographed on 27th September 1958. (E.Wilmshurst)

76.   Another eastward view shows the junction details in April 1966. The Met loop line had been on the extreme right. Local goods services were withdrawn on 6th January 1964. The box had a 40-lever frame. (J.C.Gillham)

WINSLOW

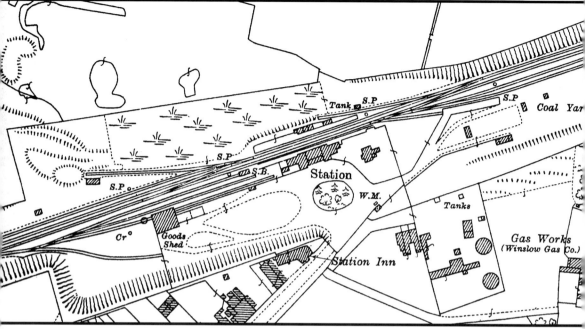

XVI.   The 1925 map shows an unusual arrangement: a coal yard on the right and a goods yard on the left. Its crane was of 5-ton capacity. The gasworks (right) was built in 1880 and could require 1000 tons of coal annually. It closed in August 1956. Station Inn is at the top of Station Road. The siding top left had earlier served a turntable for locomotives terminating here.

77.   This westward view is from around 1912 and includes the short up siding. The station design was similar to the one used at Bicester, but brick was employed throughout, with minor exceptions. (Lens of Sutton coll.)

78.   Banbury and Oxford portions of trains were divided and joined here, even after the opening of Verney Junction, but the practice died out in the 20th century. The photo is from June 1933. (Mowat coll./Brunel University)

79.   The town had a population of 2072 in 1961, the year in which this and the next picture were taken. A heavy freight is westbound and passes a trio of Sugg's Rochester pattern gas lamps. (Stations UK)

80.	A DMU for Bletchley calls for a couple of passengers standing near the waiting room, which shows evidence of solid fuel heating. Houses now occupy the site. (Stations UK)

81.	The chimney stacks and ridge tiles were splendid architectural details to enhance the symmetry, which is maintained by two Ford Anglias (albeit one Estate) in this 1964 view. (R.J.Essery/R.S.Carpenter)

82.	The signal box had 34 levers and closed on 31st January 1968, one month after the last passenger train had left. The yard seems busy in this view from 7th November 1964. (R.J.Essery/R.S.Carpenter)

83.	Seen on the same day is the typical LNWR goods shed, together with the 5-ton crane. Goods facilities were withdrawn on 22nd May 1967. (R.J.Essery/R.S.Carpenter)

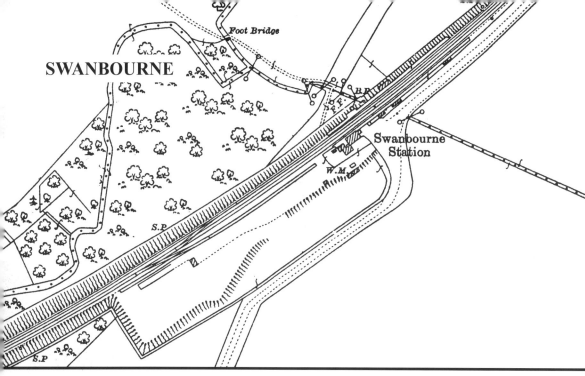

SWANBOURNE

XVII. The 1925 map shows no habitation nearby. The village was more than one mile to the south. A steep descent to Bletchley began east of this station and goods train brakes had to be pinned down on loose-coupled trains.

84.   The station may not have opened until a few months after the line, but it was never very busy; the population was 405 in 1901 and 394 in 1961. Coal was an important traffic inwards. The 10.0am Buckingham to Bletchley is seen behind a 2-6-2T no. 41275 on 19th April 1959. (H.C.Casserley)

85. The timber-clad ticket office seems to be a late addition to the house. The double gates would be opened during the transfer of goods, milk traffic in particular. The eight-lever ground frame is beyond the left gate and the instruments were in the booking office. The box closed on 27th April 1967, goods traffic having ceased on 1st June 1964. (H.C.Casserley)

86. No. 42368 is about to call with the 5.5pm Bletchley to Oxford on 4th July 1959. Of particular note is the proximity of the buildings to the down line. The parcels shed is near the engine and beyond it is the waiting room. (J.Langford)

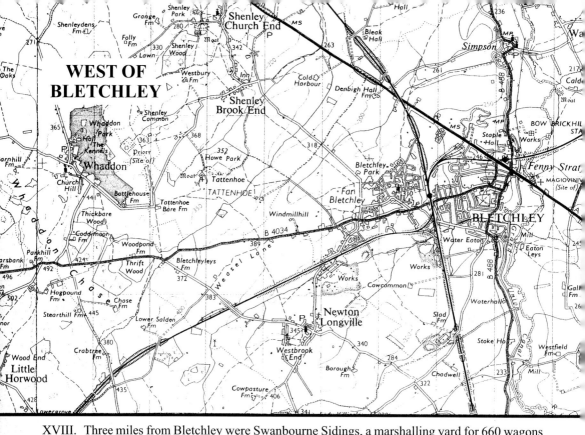

XVIII. Three miles from Bletchley were Swanbourne Sidings, a marshalling yard for 660 wagons created on the up side during World War II. Nearer were sidings on the down side for Newton Longville Brickworks. Their positions are indicated on this 1954 map at 1ins to 1 mile.

87.   Swanbourne Yard closed in March 1967, but the 30-lever box was open until 29th July 1984. (British Railways)

BLETCHLEY

88.   Trains from Oxford usually arrived at platform 2, but those going on to Cambridge ran into No. 7, beyond the train on the right. The double-headed one on the left is probably bound for Oxford. The station was rebuilt in 1881 with a roof over all tracks and platforms. (R.M.Casserley coll.)

89.   A southward view from platform 4 in 1934 includes the fast lines to London, the six-road carriage shed and the 96-lever No. 1 Box. The Oxford lines curve right beyond it. (Mowat coll./Brunel University)

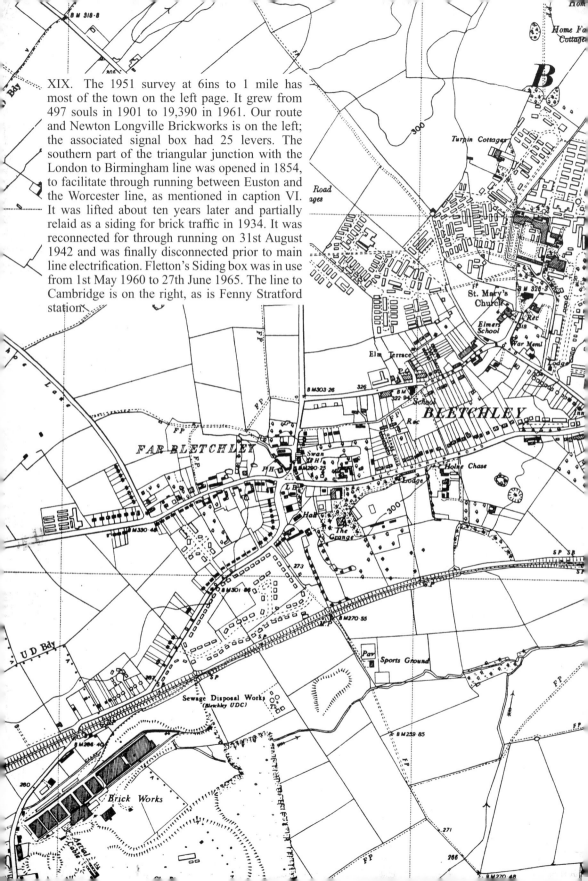

XIX. The 1951 survey at 6ins to 1 mile has most of the town on the left page. It grew from 497 souls in 1901 to 19,390 in 1961. Our route and Newton Longville Brickworks is on the left; the associated signal box had 25 levers. The southern part of the triangular junction with the London to Birmingham line was opened in 1854, to facilitate through running between Euston and the Worcester line, as mentioned in caption VI. It was lifted about ten years later and partially relaid as a siding for brick traffic in 1934. It was reconnected for through running on 31st August 1942 and was finally disconnected prior to main line electrification. Fletton's Siding box was in use from 1st May 1960 to 27th June 1965. The line to Cambridge is on the right, as is Fenny Stratford station.

90.   The main buildings are on the left as 4-4-0 no. 40743 waits to leave at 9.30am for Oxford on 23rd July 1951. (H.C.Casserley)

91.   This northward view from 7th March 1953 reveals the extent of the overall roof and the adjacent canopies. Bullhead rails were still in use. (LGRP)

92. The massive task of creating a flyover for the Oxford-Cambridge freight services began in 1958. This is the extent of progress on 4th July 1959, as no. 45184 drifted south. (H.C.Casserley)

93. We now have three photographs from 9th November 1963 showing the flyover, which was opened on 15th January 1962. In the distance are the chimneys of the mighty Fletton brickworks. (J.C.Gillham)

94.   This view is northwest along Water Eaton Road and it includes the end of the carriage shed, top right. It shows the evolution of road bridging techniques dramatically. (J.C.Gillham)

95.   All but part of the building on the right was destroyed in readiness for electrification. Part of platform 2 could still be used by DMUs from Oxford. (J.C.Gillham)

96.   This is the scene on the last day of operation to Buckingham, 5th September 1964. This route was the first to have BR's single railcars and one of the two was eventually preserved and became a resident at the Midland Railway at Butterley. This is it - no. 79900. (L.Hanson)

97.   The west side buildings were still complete when photographed in September 1964. The main lines were electrified in April 1966. (B.S.Jennings)

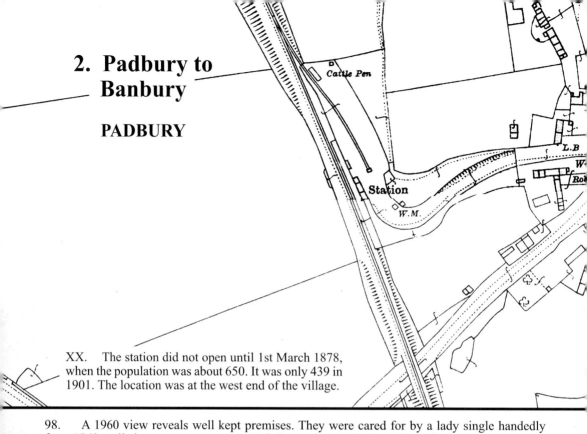

2. Padbury to Banbury

PADBURY

Cattle Pen

Station

W.M.

L.B

XX.   The station did not open until 1st March 1878, when the population was about 650. It was only 439 in 1901. The location was at the west end of the village.

98.   A 1960 view reveals well kept premises. They were cared for by a lady single handedly from 1942 until closure to passengers on 7th September 1964. (R.M.Casserley)

99.   The goods yard had been closed on 6th January 1964 and was photographed in November of that year. The cattle pen and loading gauge are almost lost in the mist. Total demolition took place in 1968 and houses were erected on the site in 1975. (R.J.Essery/R.S.Carpenter)

London & North Western Ry.
Issued subject to the conditions & regulations in the Cos Time Tables Books Bills & Notices.
WINSLOW   TO
BRACKLEY(LNW
VIA VERNEY JUNCTION
Third]   44(S)   [Class
BRACKLEY   FARE 1/2

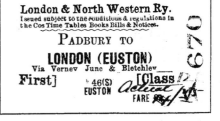

London & North Western Ry.
Issued subject to the conditions & regulations in the Cos Time Tables Books Bills & Notices.
PADBURY   TO
LONDON (EUSTON)
Via Verney Junc & Bletchley
First]   46(S)   [Class
EUSTON   FARE

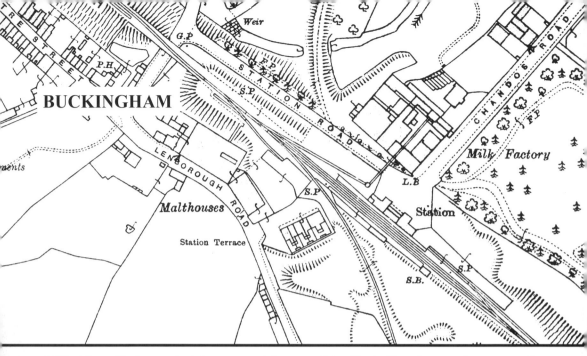

BUCKINGHAM

Weir

G.P.

STATION ROAD

CHANDOS ROAD

Milk Factory

L.B.

Station

LENBOROUGH ROAD

Malthouses

Station Terrace

S.P.

S.B.

S.P.

XXI. The milk factory had been created in part of the Castle Foundry premises, soon after the railway opened. The 1923 survey shows the loop, which remained after the short length of double track was truncated prior to WWII. It had necessitated two signal boxes. An oil depot was established here in the late 1920s. The town declined from about 4000 souls in 1861 to 3152 in 1901. The milk factory siding is included.

100.   BR class 2MT 2-6-2T stands at the down platform on 28th July 1958, while propelling the 3.35pm from Bletchley to Banbury. There had been a station staff of 13 in the early 1920s. Stowe School was opened in 1923, three miles to the north. It created end of term traffic peaks, these sometimes needing 10-coach trains. (B.W.Leslie)

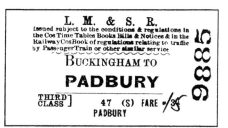

101.   The LMS erected the 28-lever signal box in 1931, following destruction of its predecessor by fire. Goods traffic ceased here on 5th December 1966, more than two years after passenger service from Bletchley. That to Banbury had ended in 1961, but through goods trains continued until 5th December 1963, mainly for cattle and ironstone. This view is from 1955. (R.M.Casserley)

102.   Similarities to Bicester are evident in this 1956 northward view. Steps in the platform brickwork were provided for staff to take a short cut over the tracks, as seen in the previous photo. (R.M.Casserley)

103.   The down side was photographed in 1964. During the partial dieselisation period in the late 1950s, some steam services from Bletchley would terminate at this platform, while railcars from Banbury would use the other one. Passengers would transfer via the crossing seen above. (R.J.Essery/R.S.Carpenter)

RADCLIVE HALT

104.   This halt came into use with the railcar service on 13th August 1956 and remained open until line closure on 2nd January 1961. It was 1¼ miles from Buckingham. (H.C.Casserley)

105.   The guard was responsible for the oil lamp lighting. There was a similar platform to this at Water Stratford, 1½ miles west. It was in use between the same dates. (H.C.Casserley)

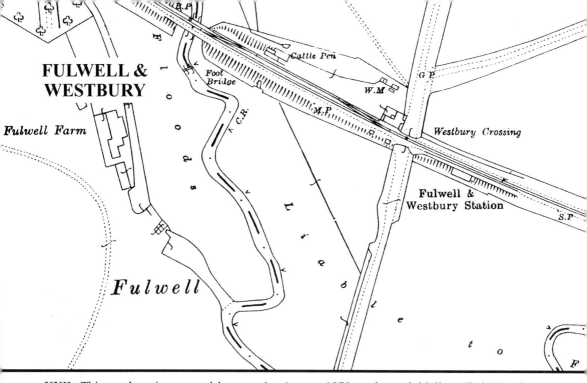

FULWELL &
WESTBURY

Fulwell Farm

Cattle Pen

Foot
Bridge

G.P.

W.M.

C.R.

M.P.

Westbury Crossing

Fulwell &
Westbury Station

S.P.

Fulwell

Lia ... b ... le ... e ... t ... o ... F

XXII. This rural station opened late, on 1st August 1879, and was initially called "Westbury Crossing". The village was one mile to the north.

106.   The gates were protected by signals operated by the crossing keeper. There were gates at only one other crossing on the branch; the other was one mile eastwards at Bacon's House, where a siding was provided south of the line. It was used for coal mainly. The photo is from March 1955. (R.M.Casserley)

107.   The house was occupied by a stationmaster until 1930 and thereafter by other staff. There were two porters here in the 1930s and one woman subsequently. Derelict in this 1966 view, the building was later restored as a dwelling. (R.M.Casserley)

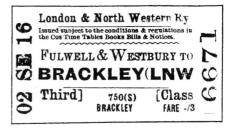

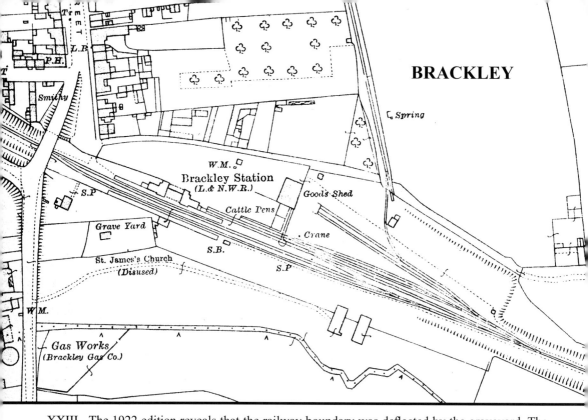

BRACKLEY

XXIII. The 1922 edition reveals that the railway boundary was deflected by the graveyard. The population increased during the life of the line from 2277 to 3610. The track at the top of the map continued to the Hopkin & Norris brewery, up at 1 in 20. Horses were employed in that direction and gravity in the other, but the siding was not used after the early 1920s. The crane was of 5-ton capacity and is shown close to the wagon turntable.

108.   The crane is visible as class 4F 0-6-0 no. 44447 arrives with three non-corridor coaches forming the 2.13pm Bletchley to Banbury service on 16th January 1954. The gasworks (lower left on the map) could demand up to 12 wagons of coal daily. It closed in October 1954. (N.W.Sprinks)

109.   The standard Buckinghamshire Railway plans were employed, but the ornamental ridge tiles were more durable here. The photographer's Hillman Minx adorns this 1958 view. Steane Park was two miles northwest and it had a private halt in the early years. (H.C.Casserley)

110.   The goods yard closed and through freight traffic ceased on 2nd December 1963, almost three years after the last passenger had left. Lack of signs and seats suggests that no. 75014 was photographed in that period. (T.J.Edgington coll.)

111.   The signal box had 20 levers and was recorded in 1964 as the grass lengthened. The suffix "Town" was added to the name on 1st July 1950, but curiously only for goods traffic. (R.J.Essery coll./R.S.Carpenter)

112.   The low platform remained to the end and is seen in 1966. An 0-6-0 diesel from the nearby depot of R.Fenwick & Co. departed for Bletchley on 16th February 1966 and was the last movement by rail. Brackley North, on the ex-GCR line, closed that year. (R.M.Casserley)

NORTH OF BRACKLEY

113. This east-ward view of the symmetrical junction at Cockley Brake has our route on the right and the line to Towcester on the left. The first signal box was in use from 1872 to 1922. The second closed in 1953 with the Towcester line; its passenger service ceased in 1951. (LGRP)

FARTHINGHOE

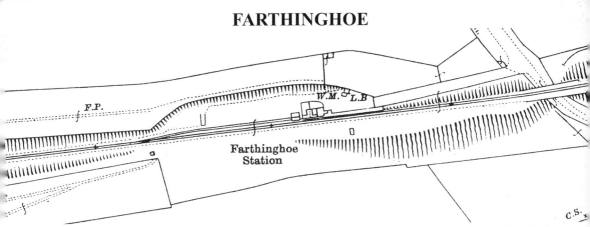

XXIV. The 1922 survey shows no habitation in the vicinity. The station opened in October 1851 and lost its passenger service on 3rd November 1952. Goods facilities remained until line closure on 2nd December 1963.

114. A 1955 record from a passing train reveals that the booking office and toilets were timber clad. There was one man here until 1963, when the place became derelict; demolition followed. (R.M.Casserley)

EAST OF BANBURY

XXV. The Ministry of Munitions established an extensive depot 1½ miles from the town centre in 1916 and it is shown on the 1922 survey at 12ins to 1 mile. The line at the top branched into two and continued to serve three remote stores. The filling sheds are connected by two-foot gauge tracks on which the wagons were hand propelled. At cessation of production in 1919, there was an 0-6-0ST and an 0-4-0T on site, together with some 2000 staff. Closure was in 1924, but the area was used again in the next conflict.

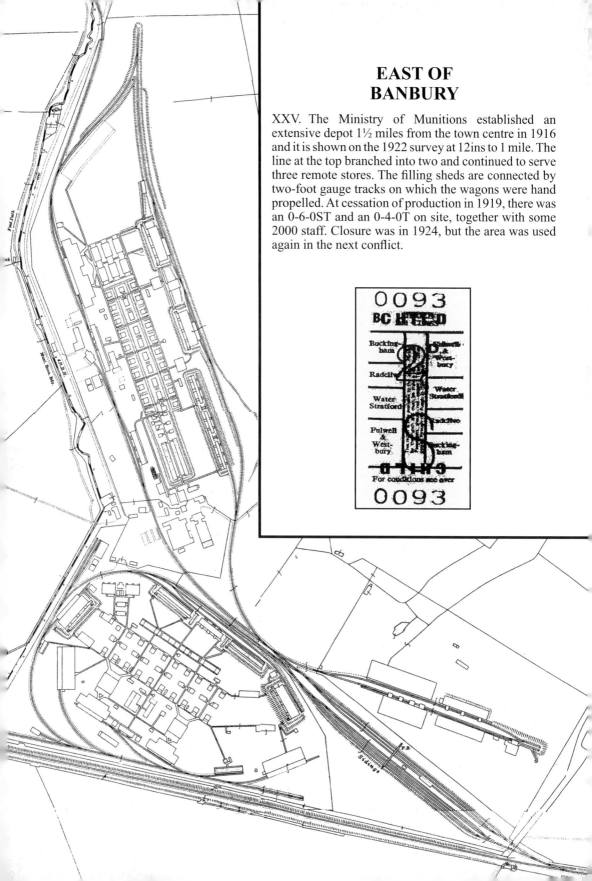

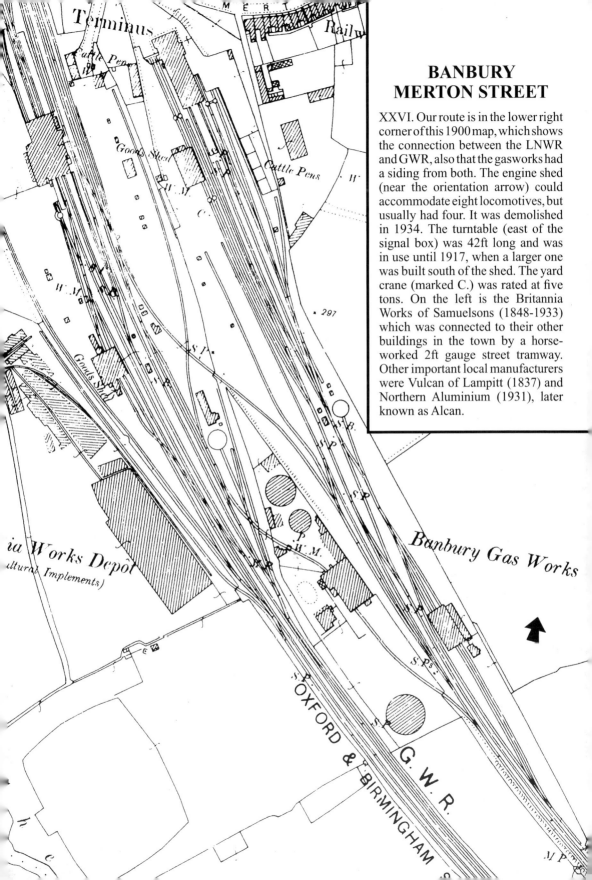

BANBURY
MERTON STREET

XXVI. Our route is in the lower right corner of this 1900 map, which shows the connection between the LNWR and GWR, also that the gasworks had a siding from both. The engine shed (near the orientation arrow) could accommodate eight locomotives, but usually had four. It was demolished in 1934. The turntable (east of the signal box) was 42ft long and was in use until 1917, when a larger one was built south of the shed. The yard crane (marked C.) was rated at five tons. On the left is the Britannia Works of Samuelsons (1848-1933) which was connected to their other buildings in the town by a horse-worked 2ft gauge street tramway. Other important local manufacturers were Vulcan of Lampitt (1837) and Northern Aluminium (1931), later known as Alcan.

115.   Two photographs from 15th March 1952 show the roof intact. This one also includes the gas holders, the ex-LNWR goods shed and the weighing machine office. There were through coaches from here to Euston in 1901-16. (H.C.Casserley)

116.   The 3.42pm to Bletchley that day was hauled by 2-6-4T no. 42669. The line of cattle wagons is a reminder of the great importance of this traffic on the route. (H.C.Casserley)

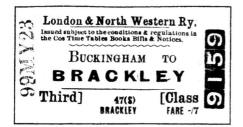

117.   This northward view from the early 1930s includes wagons lettered BANBURY GAS Co. in the coal stock yard.The LMS goods shed is on the extreme right. The works was in use from 1856 until 1958. (Banbury Gas Co.)

118.   The roof sheeting was removed for safety reasons in 1955 and the remaining structures were painted. No. 1 platform (right) had usually been used for Blisworth trains (until 1951), no. 2 normally being for Bletchley services. (R.M.Casserley)

119.   The line in the foreground continued on the right to the goods yard, which was in use until 6th June 1966. The box had 35 levers. (R.S.Carpenter)

120.   The low timber platform and gas lights contrast with the new image of a railcar on 5th September 1956. Beeching's plan would eventually be implemented and all would be lost. (B.S.Jennings)

MP Middleton Press

EVOLVING THE ULTIMATE RAIL ENCYCLOPEDIA

Easebourne Lane, Midhurst, West Sussex.
GU29 9AZ   Tel:01730 813169

www.middletonpress.co.uk   email:info@middletonpress.co.uk

A-0 906520   B-1 873793   C-1 901706   D-1 904474

OOP Out of Print at time of printing - Please check current availability   **BROCHURE AVAILABLE SHOWING NEW TITLES**